Analogue Guide

Amsterdam

Contents

Amsterdam

—Welcome to Analogue Amsterdam

Despite its modest size and location below sea level, Amsterdam has established itself as one of Europe's most important cities. Much of this can be attributed to its liberal disposition, which once made it a haven for persecuted minorities and intellectuals, and more recently a magnet for tourists and expats.

Founded in 1204 on a dam on the river Amstel, Amsterdam's history is closely intertwined with the battle against the sea—a hands-on enterprise which fostered a sense of individual responsibility. By the 16th century, the traders of Amsterdam had found a lucrative niche in the pepper trade, soon turning the city into Europe's dominant trading hub. Amsterdam's freewheeling atmosphere provided an intellectual breeding ground where censorship was unheard of. Though the city eventually had to share the spoils of globalisation with others, Amsterdam has preserved much of its open-minded attitude—to a degree more typically found in the New World than in Europe—and today is a crossroads of commerce, people and ideas spanning the globe.

Though Amsterdam is still much associated with hordes of rain-gear clad tourists looking to catch a glimpse of its freewheeling ways, efforts have been made to rein in the excesses. The De Wallen red-light district has seen a new wave of civic life, including the emergence of boutiques and design outlets. In the city's inner west, young professionals have carved out an urban way of life beyond the well-trodden paths of the picturesque canal belt. Amsterdam has also recently discovered its "wild north" on the opposite bank of the IJ lake, where warehouses provide new space for artists and creative types. We've set out to discover the best that this maritime city has to offer, from the classic highlights of the Canal Belt to the neighbourhood treasures beyond. Enjoy!

Neighbourhoods

Oud-West –p78
Popular with young professionals and families, the Oud-West offers Amsterdam canal-side lure in a low-key setting

Jordaan –46
Arguably Amsterdam's most charming neighbourhood, the Jordaan's small alleys are lined with small shops, galleries and ateliers

Canal Belt –p8
Amsterdam's famous canals and the mansions of old merchant families now house upmarket retail, hotels and galleries

Oud-Zuid –p72
The Oud-Zuid's leafy streets are home to the city's professional classes, as well as many of Amsterdam's world class museums

WESTERPARK

JORDAAN

OUD-WEST

CA

OUD-ZUID

N

2 kilometres

AMSTERDAM-ZUID

SCHIPHOL-(5KM)

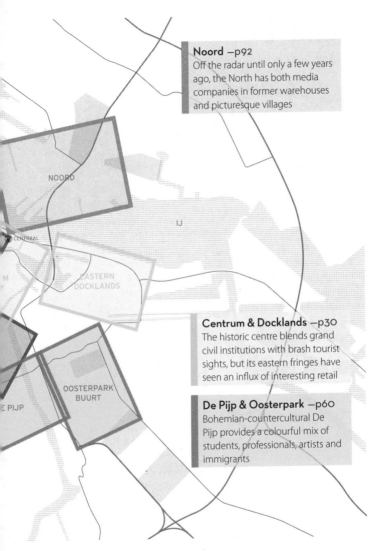

Noord —p92
Off the radar until only a few years ago, the North has both media companies in former warehouses and picturesque villages

Centrum & Docklands —p30
The historic centre blends grand civil institutions with brash tourist sights, but its eastern fringes have seen an influx of interesting retail

De Pijp & Oosterpark —p60
Bohemian-countercultural De Pijp provides a colourful mix of students, professionals, artists and immigrants

NOORD

IJ

CENTRAAL

EASTERN DOCKLANDS

OOSTERPARK BUURT

E PIJP

Canal Belt

—Quintessential Amsterdam

The Canal Belt, or *grachtengordel*, accounts for much of the picturesque ideal commonly associated with Amsterdam. Overlooking the tree-lined canals are the elegant mansions of old merchant families, with their decorated gables and tall, slender windows. Cyclists hurry over low arch bridges and on summer weekends the canals teem with locals promenading their boats.

The innermost of the four major *grachten* that surround the centre, the Singel was the medieval city's moat. Buoyed by the successful spice trade underwriting the city's 17th century Golden Age, Amsterdam was bursting at the seams. A plan was drawn up to create three new canal rings, the Herengracht, Keizersgracht and Prinsengracht. Upon their completion, most of the city's wealthy merchants left the old centre, moving into the newly developed canal district, with family, warehouse and *kantoor* all housed under the same roof and directly accessible from the canals by barge. At the same time, the small canals and streets linking the rings housed ancillary trades and crafts, providing the area with a diverse social mix. The build-up of the district began in the west, but by the time construction reached the Amstel river in the south, Amsterdam's fortunes had turned. This left the canals' eastern section only partially completed and dominated by public institutions, such as the botanical garden.

Today, the prestigious merchants' homes house law firms, private banks, upmarket hotels and galleries. The *Negen Straatjes*, nine of the streets linking the canal rings, boast a particularly interesting mix of independent retail and gastronomy in a picturesque setting. In the south, the *Spiegelkwartier* near the Museum Quarter (p 72) is home to numerous antique shops.

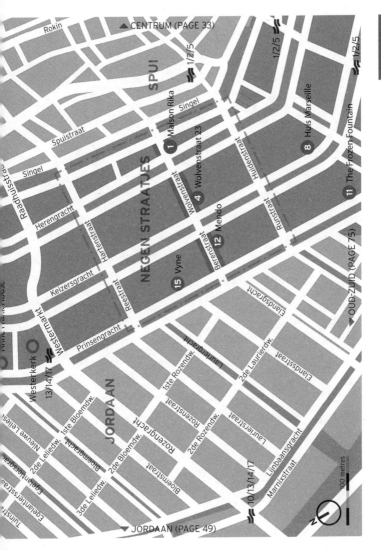

▲ CENTRUM (PAGE 33)

Rokin

Spuistraat

Singel

Singel

Raadhuisstraat

Herengracht

Keizersgracht

Prinsengracht

Westermarkt

Westerkerk

SPUI

1/2/5

1/2/5

1/2/5

Huis Marseille

The Frozen Fountain

NEGEN STRAATJES

Maison Rika

Singel

Wolvenstraat

Wolvenstraat 23

Huidenstraat

Hartenstraat

Runstraat

Berenstraat

Mendo

Reestraat

Vyne

Elandsgracht

1 Maison Rika

4 Wolvenstraat 23

8 Huis Marseille

11 The Frozen Fountain

12 Mendo

15 Vyne

► OUD-ZUID (PAGE 75)

13/14/17

JORDAAN

1ste Bloemdw.

2de Bloemdw.

Bloemgracht

Bloemstraat

3de Leliedw.

2de Leliedw.

1ste Leliedw.

Nieuwe Leliestr.

Egelantiersstr.

Tuinstr.

Egelantiersgr.

1ste Rozendw.

2de Rozendw.

Rozengracht

Rozenstraat

Lauriergracht

Laurierstraat

1ste Laurierdw.

2de Laurierdw.

Elandsstraat

Lijnbaansgracht

Marnixstraat

10/13/14/17

100 metres

N

▼ JORDAAN (PAGE 49)

▲ CENTRUM (PAGE 33)

4/9/14/16/24

Oude Turfmarkt

SPUI

Rokin

Wolvenstraat

1 Maison Rika

Singel

1/2/5

4 Wolvenstraat 23

Reguliersbree

Keizersgracht

Huidenstraat

Singel

Vijzelstraat

Reguliersdwarsstraat

1/2/5

Herengracht

16/2

8 Huis Marseille

FOAM

11 The Frozen Fountain

1/2/5 Keizersgracht

◄ JORDAAN (PAGE 49)

Leidsegracht

Leidsestraat

SOUTH

Nieuwe Spiegelstraat

Kerkstraat

1/2/5 Prinsengracht

Lijnbaansgracht

1/2/5/7/10

SPIEGELKWARTIER

Leidseplein

Lijnbaansgracht

Weteringschans

7/10 Weteringschans

N

100 metres

Stadhouderskade

▼ OUD-ZUID (PAGE 75)

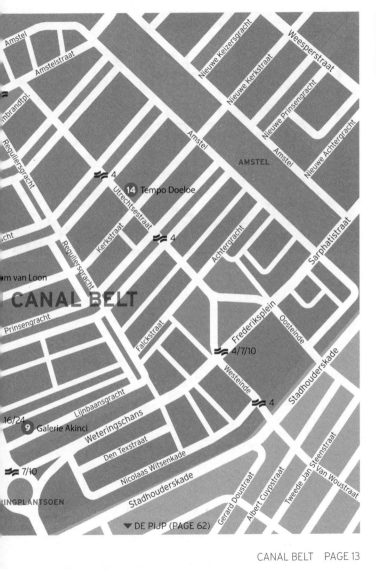

Amstel

Amstelstraat

nbrandtpl.

Reguliersgracht

Nieuwe Keizersgracht

Weesperstraat

Nieuwe Kerkstraat

Nieuwe Prinsengracht

Nieuwe Achtergracht

Amstel

AMSTEL

Amstel

≋ 4

14 Tempo Doeloe

Utrechtsestraat

Kerkstraat

≋ 4

Achtergracht

Sarphatistraat

cht

Reguliersgracht

m van Loon

CANAL BELT

Prinsengracht

Falckstraat

Frederiksplein

Oosteinde

≋ 4/7/10

Westeinde

Stadhouderskade

≋ 4

16/24

Lijnbaansgracht

9 Galerie Akinci

Weteringschans

Den Texstraat

Nicolaas Witsenkade

Stadhouderskade

Gerard Doustraat

Albert Cuypstraat

Tweede Jan Van Woustraat

≋ 7/10

INGPLANTSOEN

▼ DE PIJP (PAGE 62)

Nordic Chic

Maison Rika

 Oude Spiegelstraat 12
+31 20 330 1112
rikaint.com
Spui **1** **2** **5**
Doubles from €210/night incl. tax

Maison Rika's gracht-side location at the heart of the fashionable Nine Streets area and its Scandinavian sensibility make for an alluring Amsterdam home. The bijou guesthouse incarnation of Swedish stylist-turned-designer Ulrike Lundgren, the hotel's two rooms are decorated in a mix of rock star chic and Nordic understatement. Both have stellar views of the historical canals, and are meticulously appointed with custom pieces assembled from Ulrike's travels, fresh cut flowers and art books. Don't miss Rika, the standout fashion boutique across the canal.

Gracht-side Hotel

Canal House Hotel

2 Keizersgracht 148
+31 20 622 5182
canalhouse.nl
Westermarkt **13** **14** **17**
Doubles from €232/night incl. tax

An elegant boutique hotel composed of attractive gracht-side seventeenth century merchant's houses, the Canal House allows for the comforts and conveniences of modern living in a historic and central setting. In keeping with local traditions, the plush velvet-and-silk laden rooms are decorated in the light and dark palette of traditional Dutch painting, each quite naturally accented with a pink tulip. Some have direct views onto the canal or of the hotel's beautiful garden.

A Cosy Apartment

Kien

3 2e Weteringdwarsstraat 65
+31 20 428 5262

marykien.nl

Weteringcircuit **7** **10** **16** **24**

Doubles from €145/night incl. tax

Fancy your own Amsterdam apartment? Then Kien is just the place. Located on a peaceful, rosebush-lined street at the throbbing heart of the city, the guesthouse offers two comfortably minimalist rooms, one with a garden, the other with a balcony. Glorious canals and many of Amsterdam's attractions are but steps away. A top-notch option for the independent sort of traveller, breakfast is included; but you'll have to make it yourself!

Cosmopolitan Café

Wolvenstraat 23

 Wolvenstraat 23
Spui **1** **2** **5**
Open daily. Mon-Fri 8am-1am; Sat/
Sun 9am-3am

A convivial café/restaurant/bar, Wolvenstraat 23 and its dimly lit, sit-on-the-steps atmosphere has long attracted Amsterdam's hip and cosmopolitan crowd. An excellent lunch option, offering everything from Asian inspired salads to the classic Amsterdam "toastie" (melted cheese sandwich), Wolvenstraat is also the ideal neighbourhood espresso-stopover and an inspiring setting for that afterhours Martini.

Café Living Room

Vinnies Deli

 Haarlemmerstraat 46
+31 20 771 3086
vinniesdeli.nl
Martelaarsgracht **1** **2** **5** **13** **17**
Open daily. Mon-Fri 7.30am-6pm; Sat
9am-6pm; Sun 9.30am-6pm

For a break from bustling Haarlemmerstraat, pop into the comfy Dutch and Danish inspired vintage living room that is Vinnies Deli. Organic, sustainable and fair trade delights, the likes of homemade carrot cake and granola, are perfectly paired with Bocca Coffee Roaster's Gusto blend of Ethiopian and Brazilian beans. Drop in for breakfast, lunch or afternoon tea and leave stunningly refreshed.

Cutting Edge Photography

FOAM

 Keizersgracht 609
+31 20 551 6500

foam.org

Keizersgracht **16** **24**

Open daily. Mon-Wed/Sat/Sun 10am-6pm; Thu/Fri 10am-9pm

Admission €9.50

An exhibition space focusing on all things photographic, FOAM is also a major forum for photographers, picture editors and designers. The gallery's elegant canal-side Keizersgracht setting is the perfect backdrop for the classic and cutting edge photography adorning its walls. After losing yourself in an exhibition, head to FOAM Café and its long reading table for a tantalising fusion of Greek and Japanese cuisines in a creative setting.

Vestiges of the Spice Trade

Museum van Loon

7 Keizersgracht 672
+31 20 624 5255
museumvanloon.nl
Keizersgracht **16** **24**
Open daily 11am-5pm
Admission €8

Sitting elegantly on the Keizersgracht, the van Loon family residence offers a fascinating glimpse into Amsterdam's history. In 1602, Willem van Loon co-founded the Dutch East India Company, often referred to as the world's first multinational corporation. The company's highly profitable spice monopoly, sweeping quasi-governmental powers and colonial trading prowess throughout Asia were second to none until well into the 18th century. Van Loon's house, with its wealth of period pieces, art and other objects is fascinating in its relative austerity.

The Role of the Landscape

Huis Marseille

8 Keizersgracht 401
+31 20 531 8989
huismarseille.nl
Keizersgracht **1** **2** **5**
Closed Mon. Open Tue-Sun 11am-6pm
Admission €8

Huis Marseille focuses on contemporary photography exploring how the landscape unfurls within images. The museum is divided into six exhibition spaces but maintains the warmth of the original gabled Keizersgracht structure housing it. The residence was built in the mid-17th century for the French merchant Isaac Focquier and takes its name from the tablet he added to the facade, depicting the port of Marseille, from which he embarked upon his Dutch adventure to riches.

New Media Explored

Galerie Akinci

9 Lijnbaansgracht 317
+31 20 638 0480
akinci.nl
Weteringcircuit **7** **10** **16** **24**
Closed Mon. Open Tue-Sun 1pm-6pm

At the forefront of Amsterdam's contemporary art scene, Galerie Akinci has a mandate to present works by artists experimenting in new media. The gallery's high calibre exhibitions, such as the recent *Memory Material*, are complemented by lectures exploring the themes grappled with by artists today, such the limitations of photography and film in recuperating memory.

Functionality Meets Beauty

Property Of ...

 Herenstraat 2
+31 20 622 5909
thepropertyof.com
Nieuwezijds Kolk **1** **2** **5** **13** **17**
Open daily. Mon/Tue noon-6pm;
Wed-Sat 11am-6.30pm; Sun noon-
5pm

Property Of…offers a refined contemporary collection of bags and accessories for the sophisticated urbanite and traveller. Its dark painted wood, subway and chess-board-tiled Amsterdam boutique is bolstered by a first rate coffee bar, offering the perfect pick-me-up to prime you for the purchase of a must-have duffel bag. The bags meld functionality with clean, beautiful designs, making use of prime materials such as waxcloth, vegetable-died leather and distressed cotton canvas.

Original Crafts

The Frozen Fountain

11 Prinsengracht 645
+31 20 622 9375

frozenfountain.nl

Raamplein **7** **10**,
Prinsengracht **1** **2** **5**

Open daily. Mon 1pm-6pm; Tue-Fri
10am-6pm; Sat 10am-6pm; Sun
noon-5pm

A wondrous repository of furniture, fabrics, home accessories and arts, The Frozen Fountain is Amsterdam's creative fount of desirable objects. Founder Dick Dankers opened the store in 1985, with the intention of bringing together designers and craftspeople to present a highly original collection, with a particular specialisation in laquerwork and its application to unique, older furniture. Today, international furniture brands, classic and contemporary, meld with textiles by Hay and lamps by Studio Ilse. The Frozen Fountain also hosts exhibitions and carries a range of design related books.

Book Candy

Mendo

 Berenstraat 11
+31 20 612 1216

mendo.nl

Martelaarsgracht **1 2 5 13 17**,
Westermarkt **13 14 17**

Open daily. Mon-Sat 10.30am-6pm;
Sun noon-5pm

A "book candy" store, Mendo offers a chocolate box array of the most stunning fashion, photography, architecture, interiors, travel, food and graphic design publications around. The space itself, designed by Amsterdam's Concrete Architectural Associates, is playfully cocktail-bar-chic and lined with black covered Mendo books substituting for bricks. Founders Roy Rietstap, Joeri Worm and Joost Albronda's backgrounds in advertising and graphic design are perfectly mirrored in the shop's balance of fashion and attention to detail.

Natural Pampering

Cosmetics & Care

13 Herenstraat 30 A
+31 20 627 6732
cosmeticsandcare.com
Nieuwezijds Kolk **1** **2** **5** **13** **17**
Shop: Closed Sun/Mon. Open Tue-Sat 10am-6pm
Spa: Closed Mon. Open Tue 10am-8pm; Wed/Fri/Sat 10am-6pm; Thu 10am-9pm; Sun noon-4pm

Cosmetics & Care stocks a comprehensive range of natural health and beauty products and offers treatments such as facials and massages at its zen-like Herenstraat location. From makeup by Dutch natural cosmetics brand Be Mineral, to the latest hi-tech serum by Pure Altitude, you'll be sure to leave with the potential for total revitalisation. Cosmetics & Care also carries several options for the male aesthete, as well as the organic baby.

Indonesian Cuisine

Tempo Doeloe

14 Utrechtsestraat 75
+31 20 625 6718
tempodoeloerestaurant.nl
Keizersgracht ▣
Closed Sun. Open Mon-Sat 6pm-midnight

Ring the front door bell at Tempó Doeloe, "the good old days" in Indonesian, and enter a delicious universe governed by a tempo a little slower than that of the present day. This enchanted restaurant is an Amsterdam classic, bringing the best of Indonesian cuisine to delight the palates of the city's denizens. Among the kitchen's repertoire are the favourites *Ajam Roedjak* (chicken spiced with coconut cream and chili peppers) and *Oedang Piendang Koening* (jumbo shrimp in a sweet and sour sauce with lemongrass). The unique setting is dark-wood-crystal-and-velvet colonial.

Oenological Treasures

Vyne

 Prinsengracht 411
+31 20 344 6408

vyne.nl

Westermarkt **13** **14** **17**

Open daily. Mon-Thu 6pm-midnight;
Fri/Sat 5pm-1am; Sun 4pm-10pm

Serial-restaurateur Bert van der Leden's sleek and contemporary wine bar Vyne brings a knockout selection of oenological treasures to the Prinsengracht. Lined with a wall-to-wall climate control fridge exposing hundreds of must-drink bottles, the space inspires Amsterdammers to brush up on their knowledge of world appellations while nibbling on a range of *amuses-gueules*, from crostini to smoked eel.

Centrum & Docklands

—Historic Centre & Red-Light District

Amsterdam's historic centre, delimited by the Singel, the innermost ring canal, provides a mix of grand civil institutions, brash tourist sights, middle class retail outlets, and the sleazy characters attracted by Amsterdam's permissiveness. The area can be roughly divided into three parts: the *New Side* in the west, the *Old Side* with its famous *De Wallen* red-light district, and further east, the *Nieuwmarkt*, historically an immigrant neighbourhood.

Amsterdam's historic core is Dam square, where the Amstel river was interrupted by the dam, giving the city its name. Originally a Catholic pilgrimage centre, the city's centre was dominated by monasteries and other clerical buildings until the "Alteration" of 1578 when Amsterdam became Protestant. The area's lower reaches near the port became the haunt of sailors in pursuit of good times after months at sea, a legacy that has survived in the *De Wallen* red-light district. In the 17th century, as wealthy merchants moved into the new Canal District (p8), the area's eastern fringes around the *Nieuwmarkt* and beyond were taken over by immigrants, especially the thriving Jewish community around Waterlooplein. The *New Side* in the west saw its canals closed up in the late 19th century, making it less charming than its red-light counterpart.

Today, much of Amsterdam's centre is dominated by a mix of mid-range retail and tourism, interspersed with sophisticated pockets, such as the city's literary centre around the Spui square. The red-light district has seen an influx of interesting small shops and galleries. Further east, the city's eastern docklands were redeveloped into an upmarket residential neighbourhood peppered with hotels and restaurants in former port buildings.

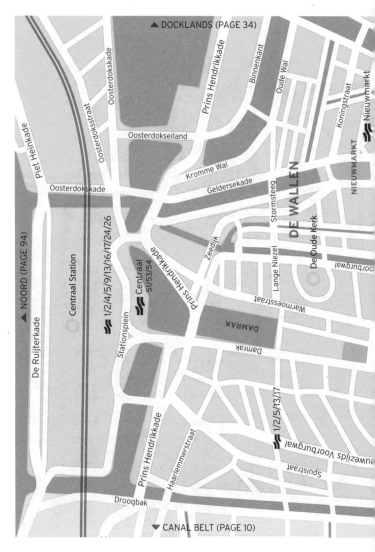

Jodenbreestraat

OUDE ZIJDE

CENTRUM

eestraat

3 Koko Coffee & Design

Kloveniersburgwal

4 WonderWood

Damstraat

Warmoesstraat

Rokin

Nieuwezijds Voorburgwal

Spuistraat

Singel

Paleisstraat

Royal Palace
🚋 1/2/5/13/14/17

DE NIEUWE KER

2 Hotel Droog

Amstel

Grimburgwal

🚋 4/9/14/16/24

Oude Turfmarkt

7 Nijhof & Lee @ Bijzondere Collecties

Rokin

SPUI

6 Athenaeum
🚋 1/2/5

Amstelstraat

Rembrandtpl.

Reguliersgracht

🚋 4/9/14

Reguliersbreestraat

Herengracht

Vijzelstraat

Reguliersdwarsstraat

Singel

🚋 1/2/5

▼ CANAL BELT (PAGE 12)

Singel

Huidenstraat

100 metres

N

▼ CANAL BELT (PAGE 11)

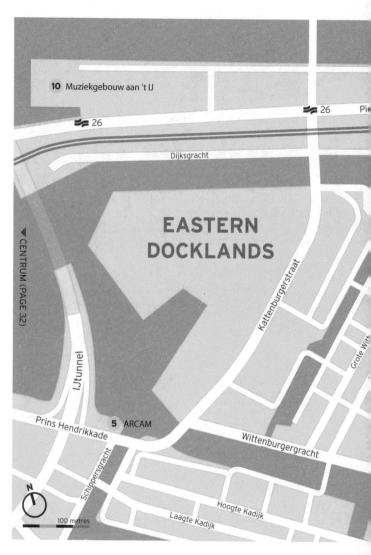

10 Muziekgebouw aan 't IJ

🚟 26

🚟 26　Pie

Dijksgracht

EASTERN DOCKLANDS

Kattenburgerstraat

Grote Witt

◀ CENTRUM (PAGE 32)

IJtunnel

Prins Hendrikkade

5 ARCAM

Wittenburgergracht

Schippersgracht

N

100 metres

Hoogte Kadijk

Laagte Kadijk

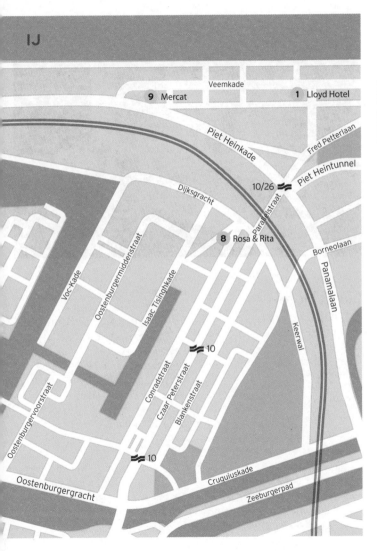

IJ

9 Mercat
1 Lloyd Hotel
Veemkade
Piet Heinkade
Fred Petterlaan
Piet Heintunnel
Dijksgracht
10/26
Paralstraat
8 Rosa & Rita
Borneolaan
Voc-kade
Oostenburgermiddenstraat
Isaac Tisinghkade
Panamalaan
Keerwal
10
Conradstraat
Czaar Peterstraat
Blankenstraat
Oostenburgervoorstraat
10
Oostenburgergracht
Cruquiuskade
Zeeburgerpad

Docklands Splendour

Lloyd Hotel

 Oostelijke Handelskade 34
+31 20 561 3636
lloydhotel.com
C. van Eesterenlaan **10**,
Rietlandpark **26**
Doubles from €69/night (one star) to
€211/night (five stars) incl. tax

While just a short tram ride from Central Station, Lloyd Hotel's distinctly maritime Eastern Docklands location and grandiose 1920s architecture feel worlds away. Inaugurated as a luxury emigrant hotel in 1920, the Lloyd subsequently did a stint as a prison, and was one of the first youth detention centres in the world, before morphing into artist's studios in the 90s. After a complete transformation by MVRDV Architects, Lloyd Hotel re-opened in 2004 as the first 1-to-5 star hotel in the world, including a "Cultural Embassy" hosting events and exhibitions.

Design Fairy Tale

Hotel Droog

 Staalstraat 7B
+31 20 523 5059
droog.com
Rembrandtplein 4 9 14
Closed Mon. Open Tue-Sun 11am-6pm

Providing 700 square metres of well-designed amusement in a gorgeous 17th century setting, Droog's design store, gallery, dining room, "fairy tale" garden, beauty and fashion centres and one unique bedroom provide the cultured hedonist's answer to a rainy day. Pop in to the Weltevree space to discover some of the marvels of contemporary Dutch outdoor design, including the iconic Dutchtub, ingeniously conceived for outdoor bathing in less than spectacular weather. The café, with its perky sofas and views over the garden, is the perfect spot to kick back with magazine and macchiato.

Stylish Coffee

Koko Coffee & Design

 Oudezijds Achterburgwal 145
+31 20 626 4208

ilovekoko.com

Nieuwmarkt **51** **53** **54**, Dam **4** **9** **16** **24**
Closed Mon. Open Tue-Fri 9.30am-6.30pm; Sat 10am-6pm; Sun noon-6pm

If you enjoy dabbling in fashion and design while you sip your espresso, Koko is the place for you. Koko curates a range of men and women's fashion and design from Scandinavia and the Netherlands, and also famously serves delectable organic brew by Antwerp's micro-roaster and coffee bar Caffènation. Located in the heart of the De Wallen red-light district, Koko is symptomatic of the area's shift towards a greater diversification of trades.

Versatile Wood

WonderWood

 Rusland 3
+31 20 625 3738
wonderwood.nl
Spui 4 9 14 16 24
Closed Sun-Tue. Open Wed-Sat
noon-6pm

WonderWood is a purveyor of the finest in plywood furniture, both vintage and contemporary. Aside from its stunning collection of 40s, 50s and 60s classic plywood chairs and re-editions by the likes of designers Marcel Breuer, Hans Brattrud and Egon Eiermann, WonderWood also displays and sells examples of wood used in art, design and gadgets. After browsing through this elegant forest, make your way to nearby Nijhof & Lee (p42) to read up on the history of chair design.

Amsterdam's Architecture

ARCAM

 Prins Hendrikkade 600
+31 20 620 4878
arcam.nl
Mr. Visserplein 9 14
Closed Sun/Mon. Open Tue-Sat
1pm-5pm
Free admission

ARCAM, the Amsterdam Centre for Architecture, was founded in 1986 with a mandate to broaden architecture's appeal to a wide range of people, while zeroing in on Amsterdam as a case study. The centre's exhibition program focuses on the city's buildings, urban planning, architects and other related topics. A permanent installation, ARCAM Panorama, provides a fascinating presentation of Amsterdam's architecture from the year 800 to the present day. Countless architecture-related publications are also made available to the public at the centre's dedicated information point.

The Athens of Amsterdam

Athenaeum

 Spui 14-16
+31 20 514 1460

athenaeum.nl

Spui **1** **2** **5**

Bookshop: Open daily. Mon 11am-6pm; Tue/Wed/Fri/Sat 9.30am-6pm; Thu 9.30am-9pm; Sun noon-5.30pm

Newsstand: Open daily. Mon-Wed/Fri/Sat 8am-8pm; Thu 8am-9pm; Sun 10am-6pm

At the core of the bustling Spui, the city's intellectual heart, the Athenaeum bookshop and newsstand provides cosmopolitan Amsterdammers with a wealth of fiction and non-fiction in several languages. A favourite haunt of students and intellectuals, the Athenaeum stocks a remarkably wide range of academically inclined titles and one of the city's most comprehensive selections of international press.

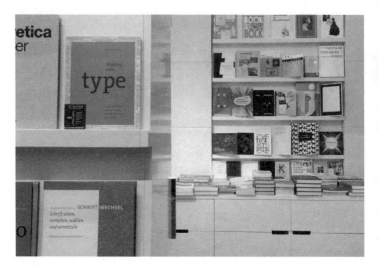

For the Visually Inclined
Nijhof & Lee @ Bijzondere Collecties

 Oude Turfmarkt 129
+31 20 525 7300
nijhoflee.nl
Spui 4 9 14 16 24
Closed Mon. Open Tue-Fri 10am-5pm; Sat/Sun 1pm-5pm

This graphic design and typography bookshop was an Amsterdam institution before it closed its doors in 2011. A compact version of the bookshop has since re-opened at the Bijzondere Collecties (Special Collections) Library of the University of Amsterdam. Specialising in the visual arts, this shop-in-library has a high-calibre selection of books on fine art, graphic design, typography, photography and architecture.

Meals on the Docks

Rosa & Rita

8 Conradstraat 471,
Oosterburgereiland
+31 6 1112 2373
rosaenrita.nl
Eerste Leeghwaterstraat **10**
Closed Mon. Open Tue-Sun from
4.30pm

Rosa & Rita infuses casual fare with a hefty dose of bonhomie, set in some grandiose shed architecture. Located at the core of Amsterdam's 17th century Eastern Docklands, the restaurant is housed in a cavernous early 20th century shipyard. Rosa and Rita were the names of two tankers manufactured for Shell in the 1930s. After stints as a photo studio, theatre workshop and garage, today's Rosa & Rita is, weather permitting, a sun-drenched spot that lends itself particularly well to summertime dinners at the outdoor tables on the terrace.

Dockside Tapas

Mercat

 Oostelijke Handelskade 4
+31 20 344 6424
mercat.nl
C. van Eesterenlaan **10**,
Kattenburgerstraat **26**
Open daily. Sun-Thu 11am-1am; Fri/
Sat 11am-2pm

Set in an Eastern Docklands warehouse, Mercat playfully adorns its bold white walls with neon signs announcing Iberian champions, the likes of *jamón* and *jerez*. Using the concept of the traditional Spanish market and its cornucopia of fresh ingredients as a starting point, chef Juan Lanzas Huitinga spins a range of contemporary and traditional Spanish dishes to a bubbly audience. Sit at the bar to explore Mercat's comprehensive wine list, tapas and *embutidos*. The terrace overlooking the water and warehouses is an excellent choice for dinner on a summer's evening.

Music on the IJ

Muziekgebouw aan 't IJ

10 Piet Heinkade 1,
+31 20 788 2000
muziekgebouw.nl
Muziekgebouw Bimhuis **26**
Regular concerts. Refer to website
for program

The Netherland's main venue
for contemporary and classical
music with a modern twist, the
Muziekgebouw benefits from
an unparalleled IJ-side location.
During the summer months,
throngs of sun-seekers line its
steps overlooking the water and
the central Amsterdam cityscape.
Cutting edge in every way, the
concert hall's ceilings, walls, chairs
and floor are all fully flexible and
moveable—allowing the space
to adapt to each performance's
specific requirements.

Jordaan
—Picturesque Boho Neighbourhood

The Jordaan, with its blend of small shops, galleries and ateliers, is arguably Amsterdam's most charming neighbourhood. Historically working class, the area has no major sights, but its labyrinth of small-scale alleys, canals and courtyards are among the city's most inviting for a picturesque afternoon stroll.

Built as part of the city's major 17th century expansion, the Jordaan was planned as a working class and immigrant district beyond the outermost ring of the Canal Belt (p8). Reflecting its early social profile, the Jordaan has a high concentration of tucked-away *hofjes* ("small courtyards")—peaceful gardens surrounded by little houses. These were commissioned by the city's wealthy merchants as alms-houses to provide shelter and protection for elderly widows. A fine example is the Karthuizerhof (see map p48).

During the industrial revolution the Jordaan became hopelessly overcrowded, prompting Amsterdam's extensive expansions in the late 19th century. In the 1970s, students and artists began to move into the decayed neighbourhood, bringing with them the boho-relaxed feel that still permeates the Jordaan today. Though no longer at the cutting edge of innovation, the Jordaan—now relatively wealthy—has retained its friendly, neighbourhoody feel. The area is dotted with *bruine* ("brown") cafés, casual gathering spots, akin to the English pub. Much neighbourhood life takes place on and round the Noordermarkt where regular food and flea markets are held.

Just to the north, Haarlemmerdijk boasts an eclectic mix of small cafés and interesting shops. The area's largely residential northern half on the other side of the rail tracks beckons for calming walks around its many canals.

▲ CANAL BELT (PAGE 10)

Herrengracht

Herenstraat

Keizersgracht

Prinsenstraat

Prinsengracht

WESTERN

N. Westerdokstraat

Haarlemmer Houttuinen

Brouwersgracht

Haarlemmerstraat

Westerdokskade

Haarlemmer Houttuinen

Haarlemmerstraat

Korte Prinsengracht

1 Finch

8 Bordewijk

NOORDER MARKT

Westerstraat

JORDAAN

1ste Anjelie

3 Headfirst Coffee

5 Restored

Brouwersgracht

1ste Goudsbloemdw.

Binnen Oranjestraat

Lindenstraat

2de Goudsbloemdw.

Karthuizerhof

Tiche

Tussen de Bogen

Vinkenstraat

Binnen Dommerssstraat

6 Concrete Matter

Haarlemmerdijk

Palmdwarsstraat

Willemsstraat

Palmstraat

3de Goudsbloemdw.

Goudsbloemstraat

Lindengracht

Haarlemmerplein

Lijnbaansgracht

Marnixstraat

Nassaukade

Haarlemmerweg

Nassaukade

De Wittenstraat

Fagelstraat

▼ WESTERPARK (PAGE 82)

PAGE 48   JORDAAN

CANAL BELT (PAGE 11)

Anne Frank House

Keizersgracht

Berenstraat

Reestraat

Prinsengracht

Westermarkt

Westerkerk

13/14/17

Nieuwe Leliestraat

Eglantiersgracht

Egelantiersstraat

Tuinstraat

Anjeliersstraat

Bloemgracht

Bloemstraat

Bloemdw.

1ste Bloemdw.

2de Bloemdw.

3de Leliedw.

2de Leliedw.

1ste Leliedw.

Lijnbaansgracht

Marnixstraat

Nassaukade

Van Oldenbarneveldtpl.

Van Oldenbarneveldtstraat

3

V. Frederik Hendrikstraat

Rombout Hogerbeetsstraat

OUD-WEST

Tweede Hugo de Grootstraat

3

Van Houweningenstraat

Yoga Garden

1ste Rozendw.

Lauriergracht

Rozenstraat

Rozengracht

7

2de Rozendw.

SPRMRKT

Bloemstraat

4

10

10/13/14/17

De Clercqstraat

OUD-WEST (PAGE 81)

Laurierstraat

1ste Laurierdw.

2de Laurierdw.

Lijnbaansgracht

Marnixstraat

Elandsgracht

Elandsstraat

9

Balthazar's Keuken

Hugo de Grootkade

100 metres

N

JORDAAN   PAGE 49

Noordermarkt Classic

Finch

 Noordermarkt 5 H
+31 20 626 2461

Nieuwe Willemsstraat **3**,
Westermarkt **13** **14** **17**

Open daily. Mon 6am-1am; Tue-Thu/
Sun 9am-1am; Fri 9am-3am; Sat
7am-3am

A Jordaan classic, Finch either ages
very well, or doesn't age at all. Set
on the picturesque Noordermarkt
square with its panoply of lively
cafés, creeping plants and flea
market on Mondays, this attractive
and dimly lit bar/café has been
luring the creatively inclined for
years. Patrons include everyone
from painters to students to
hipsters, their dogs and children.
Finch is a great place to savour an
ice-cold beer while capturing the
essence of Amsterdam's laissez-faire
spirit.

Bruin Café

Café 't Smalle

 Egelantiersgracht 12
+31 20 623 9617

t-smalle.nl

Westermarkt **13** **14** **17**,
Marnixplein **3** **10**

Open daily. Sun-Thu 10am-1am; Fri/
Sat 10am-2am

A charming canal-side *bruin* café with a quayside terrace, Café 't Smalle is a prime spot to enjoy a glass of wine or light meal after exploring the Jordaan's maze of intricate streets. Set in the 1780s distillery responsible for Peter Hoppe's famous gin, the café retains several original features, including a winding staircase, stained glass window and ornate siphon pump.

Westerstraat Espresso

Headfirst Coffee Roasters

3 Westerstraat 150
+31 6 46314112
headfirstcoffeeroasters.com
Marnixplein **3** **10**
Open daily 8am-6pm

Headfirst Coffee Roasters brings premium espresso to the heart of the Jordaan and its multiple retail offerings. The café's clean, minimal lines are softened by gorgeous flower arrangements and floor to ceiling street-side windows. While tomorrow's beans roast in the back room, sit along the banquette and enjoy some of the best coffee in town before exploring the neighbourhood.

Fashion and Pop-ups

SPRMRKT

4 Rozengracht 191
+31 20 330 5601

sprmrkt.nl

Marnixstraat/Rozengracht **10 13 14 17**

Open daily. Mon noon-6pm; Tue/
Wed/Fri/Sat 10am-6pm; Thu 10am-
8pm; Sun 1pm-6pm

A cavernous concept store on shabby-chic Rozengracht, SPRMRKT is a bit like the merger of a contemporary art gallery with an exclusive version of a New York sample sale. Featuring scores of intriguing ready-to-wear must-haves by the likes of Helmut Lang, Wood Wood and Silent by Damir Doma, SPRMRKT also sells books and plays host to art, lifestyle and pop-up events.

Unique Objects

Restored

⑤ Haarlemmerdijk 39
+31 20 337 6473

restored.nl

Haarlemmerplein ⑧

Closed Sun. Open Mon 1pm-6pm;
Tue-Fri 10am-6pm; Sat 11am-6pm

Restored curates artisanal objects carefully sourced from around the globe in a warm and attractively designed space on Haarleemerdijk. Maintaining an uncompromising focus on craftsmanship and attention to detail, the shop hunts down small label interior objects, garments and accessories by up-and-coming designers, as well as some intriguing magazines. Some of Restored's finds include Amsterdam based pottery studio J C Herman's ceramics and earthenware, Portland's Maak lab natural soaps and botanical magazine The Plant.

Gifts for the Globetrotter

Concrete Matter

6 Haarlemmerdijk 127
+ 31 20 261 0933
concrete-matter.com
Haarlemmerplein **3**
Open daily. Mon 1pm-6pm; Tue-Sat
10am-6pm; Sun noon-5pm

Against a softly lit exposed brick background, sophisticated urban males Jacob, Tomas and Tim bring you their expertly curated selection of unique and inspiring men's gifts and travel related objects. From vintage maps and botanical charts to Kaweco pen sets, Stanley flasks and a brilliantly space-efficient "flat" chess set, Concrete Matter is sure to spark the wonderlust of even the most jaded globe-trotter.

Shavasana in the Jordaan

Yoga Garden

 Eerste Rozendwarsstraat 10
yogagarden.nl

Westermarkt **13** **14** **17**

Classes from €12. Refer to website
for schedule

Situated at the back of the Health
Club Jordaan and surrounded by a
tranquil garden, Yoga Garden offers
a wide range of classes ranging
in style from Hatha to Vinyasa, Yin
Yoga and Anusara. The studio is
run as a non-profit organisation by
veteran yoga teachers Marcel van
de Vis Heil and Anat Geiger whose
aim to bring Amsterdam "a calm,
middle-sized studio for the true city
warrior" is realised with aplomb.

A Taste of the Med

Bordewijk

8 Noordermarkt 7 /HS
+31 20 624 3899
bordewijk.nl
Nieuwe Willemsstraat **3**,
Westermarkt **13 14 17**
Closed Sun/Mon. Open Tue-Sat
6.30pm-10.30pm

A stalwart on the Amsterdam foodie circuit, Bordwijk's stellar French cuisine is far from the only reason to pay a visit. In the summer months, locals flock to the terrace just off charming Noordermarkt square to sip rosé while delving into tender grilled *coquilles Saint-Jacques*. During the rest of the year, Bordewijk's modern and convivial dining room offers respite from grey skies as Mediterranean classics the likes of a top notch Bouillabaisse bring the Côte d'Azur that much closer to Benelux.

Seasonally Driven Kitchen

Balthazar's Keuken

9 Elandsgracht 108-BG
+31 20 420 2114
balthazarskeuken.nl
Elandsgracht **7** **10** **17**
Closed Sun-Tue. Open Wed-Sat
5.30pm-10.30pm

Balthazar's Keuken's quirky metropolitan flair, open kitchen and fresh international cuisine, have been delighting patrons since it opened in 1995. Chefs Karin Gaasterland and Alain Parry concoct creative seasonally driven three-course menus that change weekly. With a welcoming atmosphere conducive to lengthy conversation, the restaurant's location on bustling Elandsgracht at the heart of the Jordaan also makes this the perfect spot to round off a busy day around the *grachten*.

De Pijp & Oosterpark

—Counterculture and Ethnic Cuisine

Historically a working class neighbourhood, today's De Pijp is a colourful mix of students, professionals, artists and immigrants. Though the area has a pronounced bohemian-countercultural character throughout, urbane pockets stand out around the pleasant Sarphatipark and along the banks of the Amstel river.

De Pijp ("The Pipe", most likely for its long streets) was built in the late 19th century as one of the first neighbourhoods outside the city's canal ring (p8). Amsterdam's inner-city working class neighbourhoods, notably the Jordaan (p46), had become heavily overpopulated and social conditions were untenable. As such, few resources were put into the development of the Pijp: the land was raised for drainage, streets were built on the existing land use pattern, and houses constructed as quickly and cheaply as possible—which explains why most houses in the area look quite similar. Since the neighbourhood's early existence, social and commercial life has centred on the Albert Cuypmarkt, the largest daily market in the country, which today provides fresh ingredients to the neighbourhood's many ethnic restaurants.

Across the river Amstel in the east are the pleasant, predominantly residential neighbourhoods of Oosterparkburt and Watergraafsmeer (see map p64/65), the latter centred on Frankendael, a former estate surrounded by beautiful gardens.

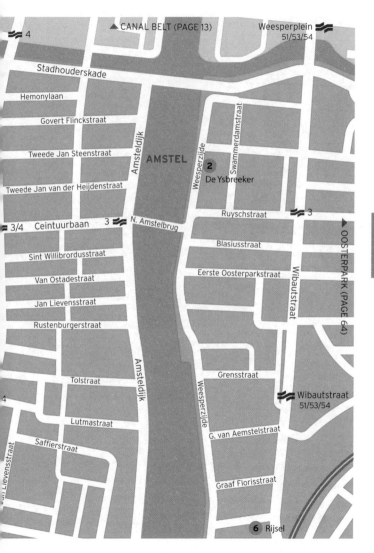

▲ CANAL BELT (PAGE 13)

Weesperplein
51/53/54

Stadhouderskade

Hemonylaan

Govert Flinckstraat

Tweede Jan Steenstraat

Tweede Jan van der Heijdenstraat

Amsteldijk

AMSTEL

Weesperzijde

Swammerdamstraat

2 De Ysbreeker

Ceintuurbaan   3

3/4

N. Amstelbrug

Ruyschstraat   3

Blasiusstraat

Eerste Oosterparkstraat

▲ OOSTERPARK (PAGE 64)

Wibautstraat

Sint Willibrordusstraat

Van Ostadestraat

Jan Lievensstraat

Rustenburgerstraat

Amsteldijk

Weesperzijde

Grensstraat

Tolstraat

4

Lutmastraat

Wibautstraat
51/53/54

G. van Aemstelstraat

Saffierstraat

Lievensstraat

Graaf Florisstraat

6 Rijsel

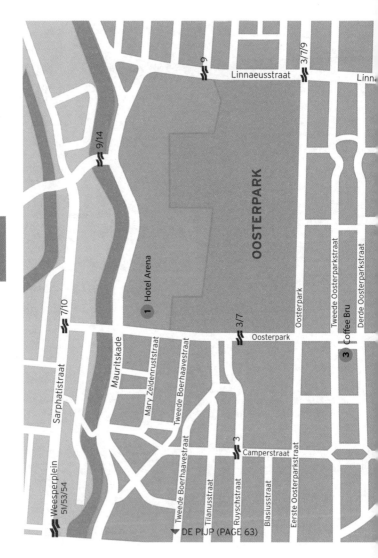

OOSTERPARK

Linnaeusstraat

Linn

3/7/9

9

9/14

7/10

Sarphatistraat

Weesperplein
51/53/54

1 Hotel Arena

Mauritskade

Mary Zeldenruststraat

Tweede Boerhaavestraat

3/7

Oosterpark

Oosterpark

Tweede Oosterparkstraat

Derde Oosterparkstraat

Coffee Bru

3

Tweede Boerhaavestraat

Tilanusstraat

Ruyschstraat

3

Camperstraat

Blasiusstraat

Eerste Oosterparkstraat

▼ DE PIJP (PAGE 63)

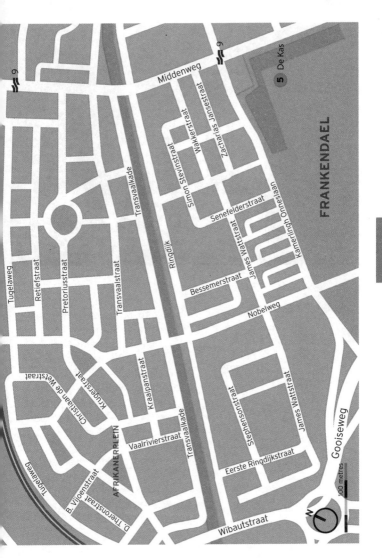

5 De Kas

Middenweg

FRANKENDAEL

Wakkerstraat

Zacharias Jansestraat

Simon Stevinstraat

Senefelderstraat

Transvaalkade

Ringdijk

James Wattstraat

Kamerlingh Onneslaan

Bessemerstraat

Tugelaweg

Retiefstraat

Pretoriusstraat

Transvaalstraat

Nobelweg

Christiaan de Wetstraat

Krugerstraat

Kraaipanstraat

Stephensonstraat

James Wattstraat

Gooiseweg

AFRIKANERPLEIN

Vaalrivierstraat

Transvaalkade

Eerste Ringdijkstraat

B. Vijoenstraat

D. Theronstraat

Tugelaweg

100 metres

N

Wibautstraat

Dutch Comfort

Hotel Arena

 's-Gravesandestraat 51
+31 20 850 2400

hotelarena.nl

Korte s'-Gravesandestraat **7** **10**

Doubles from €94/night incl. tax

Housed in a former orphanage in Amsterdam's mostly residential Oosterpark area, Hotel Arena merges Dutch efficiency with comfortable contemporary design. Rooms are decorated in natural off-white tones and accentuate original features like the building's high ceilings and wooden beams. The hotel has a restaurant specialising in Dutch cuisine, and the bar's outdoor terrace is a pleasant place to meet for a drink on a warm day. And if you're feeling sprightly, the Arena also has its own stock of bicycles reserved for guests.

Amsterdam Institution

De Ysbreeker

2 Weesperzijde 23
+31 20 468 1808

deysbreeker.nl

Wibautstraat **3**,
Weesperplein **7 10 51 53 54**

Open daily. Sun-Thu 8am-1am; Fri/
Sat 8am-2am

An Amsterdam institution on the banks of the Amstel river, De Ysbreeker has long been a favourite for brunch, coffee and late night drinks. From its large, sunny (weather permitting) riverside terrace to its elegant 18th century interior, restored with a contemporary twist, everybody who has spent some time in the city seems to be familiar with the place. Once a favourite haunt of Amsterdam's late 19th century socialist intelligentsia, the café's intellectual yet trendy atmosphere and fresh locavore cuisine now draw a highly varied crowd.

Macchiato and Banana Bread

Coffee Bru

 Beukenplein 14-H
+31 20 751 9956

Beukenweg **3** **7**

Open daily. Mon-Fri 8am-6pm; Sat/
Sun 9am-6pm

A friendly café in Amsterdam's
down-to-earth East, Coffee
Bru's macchiatos, flat whites
and espressos are a force to be
reckoned with and taste divine
with a slice of home made banana
bread. Owned by a trio of coffee
aficionados, the café's youthful
exuberance and creative energy is
tangible. If the weather is nice, take
your coffee to go on a stroll around
nearby Oosterpark.

Innovative Finds

COTTONCAKE

(4) 1e van der Helststraat 76-hs
+31 20 789 5838

cottoncake.nl

Albert Cuypstraat **16** **24**, Tweede van der Helststraat **3**

Open daily. Mon-Fri 10am-6.30pm; Sat 10am-5.30pm; Sun 11.30am-5.30pm

COTTONCAKE is at once a multi-storey apparel and home design shop and an airy café. Located at the heart of alternative de Pijp, the shop sells innovative pieces sourced from the owner's travels around the world. Textiles from Bali rub shoulders with Swedish sunglasses and Danish scarves, all displayed with laissez-faire coordination. Drop by for breakfast to sample the scrumptious oven roasted muesli with coconut and cranberry, to be enjoyed along with a cappuccino and a good read.

Greenhouse Elegance

De Kas

 Kamerlingh Onneslaan 3
+31 20 462 4562
restaurantdekas.nl
Hogeweg **9**
Closed Sun. Open Mon-Sat noon-2pm, 6.30pm-10pm

De Kas is the brainchild of Gert Jan Hageman, a Michelin star-awarded chef with a penchant for Dutch *haute cuisine*. After working in several of the city's best kitchens, Hageman decided that it was time to re-invent the conventional dining setup by moving into the greenhouse occupied by Amsterdam's Municipal Nursery since 1926. Dining under the stars in this 8-metre high glass structure, surrounded by herb and vegetable gardens, is a magical experience. The inventive, intricate and delicious fixed menu is a delight.

Scrumptious Rotisserie

Rijsel

 Marcusstraat 52
+31 20 463 2142
rijsel.com
Wibautstraat 51 53 54
Closed Sun/Mon. Open Tue-Sat from
6pm

A very high quality rotisserie, Rijsel's contemporary French/Flemish flair elevates the humble bird and its accoutrements to new heights. The simple but handsome dining room fills up quickly as *poulet et vin* inspired conversation flows throughout. Located in a former school, thick wooden floorboards, Gallic-style 50s bistro chairs and an open kitchen make Rijsel a particularly welcoming spot to spend the evening. The restaurant's name derives from the Dutch soubriquet for the French city of Lille.

Oud-Zuid

—Wealthy Upper Class Amsterdam

The Oud-Zuid ("Old South"), Amsterdam's richest neighbourhood, is the conservative heartland of the city's professional and upper classes. Its central parts are dominated by the Museumsplein and its three world-famous museums: the Rijksmuseum (p76), the Van Gogh Museum and the modern Stedelijk Museum.

The Oud-Zuid was developed in the late 19th century, in parallel to adjacent De Pijp (p60), but targeted a different audience. The same overcrowding and social blight riddling the Jordaan (p46) caused many rich Amsterdammers to leave the city for the countryside. The Oud-Zuid was thus planned as a district of stately homes, wide streets and a private park—the Vondelpark, which at the time was only accessible to members and neighbouring residents. In the same vein, the area also became the site of the Rijksmuseum, the first dedicated building for the Dutch national museum, and the Concertgebouw and its world-class resident Royal Concertgebouw Orchestra. Adjacent to the south, the residential Apollobuurt neighbourhood, designed as part of Amsterdam's major 1920s expansion, boasts a large collection of Amsterdam School style, brick expressionist architecture (see also p88).

The lively centre of the neighbourhood today is the Museumsplein and nearby P.C. Hooftstraat where—rather atypically for Amsterdam—black limousines shuttle leopard-clad ladies between the boutiques of international fashion brands. The neighbourhood's more low key and refined offerings can be found further along the Vondelpark on and around Cornelis Schuytstraat.

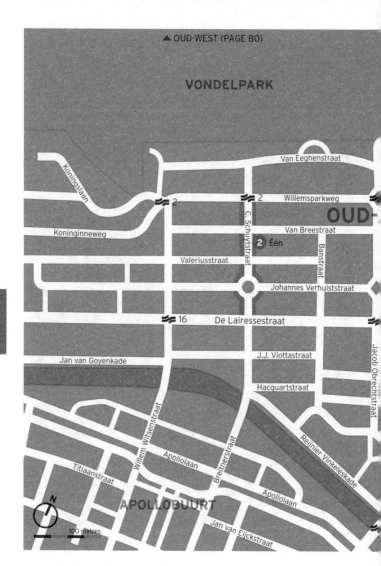

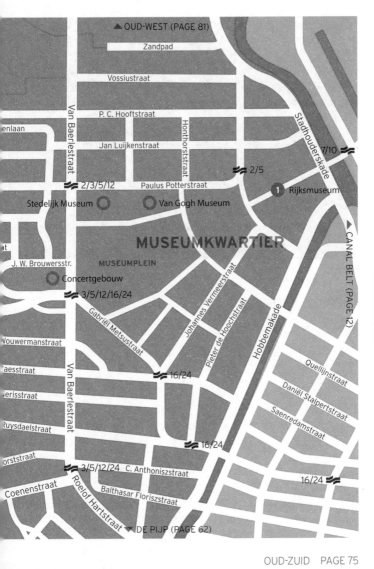

OUD-WEST (PAGE 81)

Zandpad

Vossiustraat

P. C. Hooftstraat

Jan Luijkenstraat

Honthorststraat

2/5

7/10

Stadhouderskade

enlaan

Van Baerlestraat

2/3/5/12

Paulus Potterstraat

Rijksmuseum

Stedelijk Museum

Van Gogh Museum

MUSEUMKWARTIER

MUSEUMPLEIN

t

J. W. Brouwersstr.

Concertgebouw

3/5/12/16/24

CANAL BELT (PAGE 12)

Gabriël Metsustraat

Johannes Vermeerstraat

Pieter de Hoochstraat

Hobbemakade

Vouwermanstraat

aesstraat

16/24

Quellijnstraat

erisstraat

Daniël Stalpertstraat

Ruysdaelstraat

Van Baerlestraat

16/24

Saenredamstraat

orststraat

3/5/12/24

C. Anthoniszstraat

16/24

Coenenstraat

Roelof Hartstraat

Balthasar Floriszstraat

DE PIJP (PAGE 62)

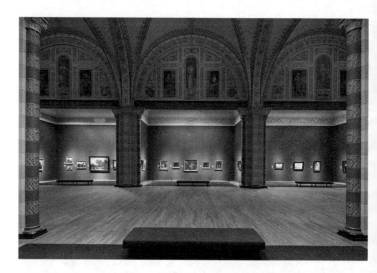

From Vermeer to Art as Therapy

Rijksmuseum

1 Museumstraat 1
+31 20 674 7000
rijksmuseum.nl
Rijksmuseum **2** **5**,
Spiegelgracht **7** **10**
Open daily 9am-5pm
Admission €15

Most of Amsterdam's renowned cultural institutions, including the Van Gogh and Stedelijk Museums, are clustered around the Museumsplein. At its heart is the recently revamped Rijksmuseum, dedicated to the art and history of the Netherlands, where paintings, applied art and history form a single time band telling the story of the nation. Exhibitions such as Alain de Botton's Art is Therapy continue the dialogue with aesthetics in a contemporary constellation. For a break, head to the Rijk's beautifully landscaped gardens, where you can enjoy a cup of tea surrounded by butterflies and botanicals.

Refined Menswear
Één

2 Cornelis Schuytstraat 19
+31 20 420 0560
1-amsterdam.nl
Cornelis Schuytstraat **2**,
Emmastraat **16**
Open daily. Mon noon-6.30pm; Tue-Fri 11am-6.30pm; Sat 10am-6pm; Sun noon-5pm

Één, "one" in Dutch, curates a range of epicurean menswear on upscale Cornelis Schuytstraat. Set amidst the leafy pavement cafés and bourgeois abodes of the classic Oud Zuid, the boutique's easy going staff, antelope head-clad walls and stage-set lighting, feels refreshingly relaxed. Brands include Maison Kitsune, Officine Generale, Porter and local arts and crafts collective Guild of Holland. For the female hedonist, visit Één's sister, Twee ("two") situated just down the street at number 27.

Oud-West

—Up-and-Coming

The Oud-West ("Old West") is perhaps the most underrated of Amsterdam's neighbourhoods. Located just outside the Jordaan (p46), the area's recent revival has been driven by young professionals and families priced out of the centre and the nearby Jordaan in particular. The calm residential area's canals are dotted with up-and-coming coffee outlets and casual restaurants.

The Oud-West was developed as a working class neighbourhood at the same time as De Pijp (p60) and upmarket Oud-Zuid (p72) in the late 19th century. The area's thoroughfare and high street, De Clercqstraat, became an axial road connecting the city's centre with its new districts in the west. The same period also saw the creation of the Westerpark, a generous green lung in an otherwise dense fabric of tenement houses and industrial installations. The adjacent enormous grounds of the former Westergasfabriek ("Western Gas Plant", p86) were converted into a cultural centre in the early 2000s, providing a great boost to the neighbourhood.

The Oud-West's main attractions can be found on or off its main thoroughfares, parallel De Clercqstraat and Kinkerstraat. The central Da Costabuurt offers the typical Amsterdam charms of canals and lift bridges in a low-key, local setting. The neighbourhood's southern fringes near the Vondelpark are more middle-class and its high street, the Overtoom, more predictable.

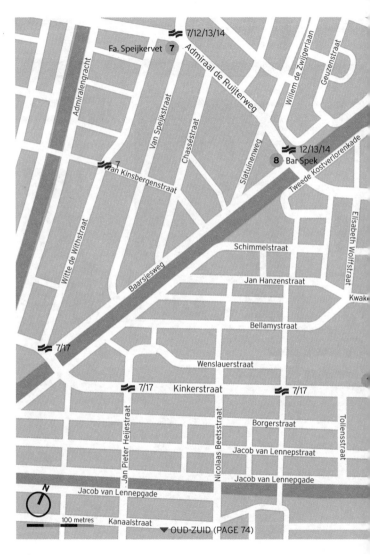

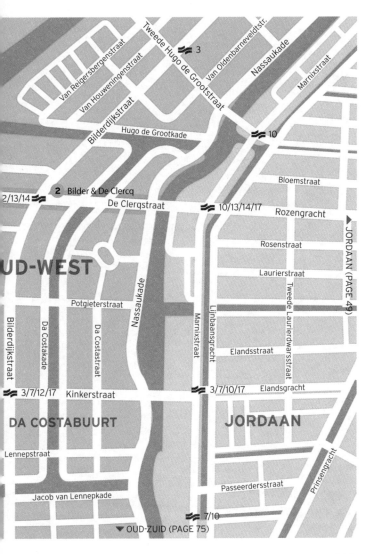

Tweede Hugo de Grootstraat

≈ 3

Van Reigersbergenstraat

Van Houweningenstraat

Van Oldenbarneveldtstr.

Nassaukade

Marnixstraat

Bilderdijkstraat

Hugo de Grootkade

≈ 10

Bloemstraat

2/13/14 ≈

2 Bilder & De Clercq

De Clercqstraat

≈ 10/13/14/17

Rozengracht

Rosenstraat

▲ JORDAAN (PAGE 49)

OUD-WEST

Laurierstraat

Tweede Laurierdwarsstraat

Potgieterstraat

Nassaukade

Lijnbaansgracht

Marnixstraat

Bilderdijkstraat

Da Costakade

Da Costastraat

Elandsstraat

3/7/12/17 ≈

Kinkerstraat

≈ 3/7/10/17

Elandsgracht

DA COSTABUURT

JORDAAN

Lennepstraat

Jacob van Lennepkade

Passeerdersstraat

Prinsengracht

≈ 7/10

▼ OUD-ZUID (PAGE 75)

Haparandaweg

6 Pont 13

IJ

Ommerdijk

Stvangerweg

Tasmanstraat

Nova Zemblastraat

Houtmankade

Houtmankade

Van Diemenstraat

Houtmankade

3

Barentszstraat

Planciusstraat

Zoutkeetsgracht

Caffeinated Excellence

Lot Sixty One

 Kinkerstraat 112
+31 6 4261 3342
lotsixtyonecoffee.com
Bilderdijkstraat/Kinkerstraat **3 7**
12 17

Open daily. Mon-Fri 8am-5pm; Sat/
Sun 10am-5pm

An in-house roasting shop, delectable flat whites and a sunny southern exposure overlooking Kinkerstraat make bijou-sized Lot Sixty One the clear choice for coffee lovers in the Oud-West. Aussie owner Adam Craig ran Variety Café in Brooklyn before deciding to make the leap over the pond and it's no surprise that he chose the rather Brooklynesque Oud-West as his location of choice. The café's name pays tribute to the lot where the coffee is grown and to the dialling code of the Down Under mecca of contemporary coffee culture.

Easy Cooking
Bilder & De Clercq

 De Clercqstraat 44
+31 20 760 7640

bilderdeclercq.nl

Bilderdijkstraat/de Clercqstraat 3
12 13 14

Open daily. Mon-Fri 8am-9pm; Sat/
Sun 10am-8pm

Overlooking De Clercqstraat's meandering tram tracks, Bilder & De Clercq is an innovative foodie concept store and café. Providing pre-measured organic ingredients to create fourteen delicious recipes, this is the place to go if you feel like cooking in. Recipes, which each come with an easy to follow recipe card, include Chermoula sausage with north African eggplant, risotto with pumpkin and sage and confit of duck. Pick up a bottle of Bilder's organic wine and you're good to go. The shop's bright and contemporary turquoise tiled café is a lovely spot to take a coffee and croissant break at any time of day.

Innovative Parklands

Westergasfabriek

3 Polonceaukade 27
+31 20 586 0710
westergasfabriek.nl
Van Limburg Stirumstraat **10**
Public access

Built as a coal gas factory complex in the 19th century, the heavily polluted Westergasfabriek ceased production in the 1960s but took out a new lease on life in the 90s as the setting for cultural and artistic activities. An immediate success with the creative, entrepreneurial and artistic set, the plant and its surrounding park were redeveloped into today's complex of innovative cafés, restaurants, galleries, shops and creative offices. The impressive structure, its cultural outposts and surrounding wildlife, make the ideal setting for a weekend stroll, followed by a strong espresso at Espressofabriek (p87).

Westergas Café

Espressofabriek

4 Pazzanistraat 39
+31 20 486 2106
espressofabriek.nl
Van Limburg Stirumstraat **10**
Open daily. Mon-Fri 9.30am-6pm;
Sat/Sun 10am-6pm

In the midst of the Westergasfabriek's (p86) grounds, enjoy
a top-notch espresso based drink
with a slice of old-fashioned
apple cake or a *tramezzino*. One
of Amsterdam's first independent
specialised cafés, Espressofabriek
is housed in one of the plant's
high ceilinged gas meter rooms,
surrounded by parkland shrubbery.
On a summer's day, grab a coffee to
go before setting out into the wilds
of the park for an idyllic picnic.

Maritime Brick Expressionism

Het Schip

 Spaarndammerplantsoen 140
+31 20 418 2885
hetschip.nl
Bus **22 48** to Oostzaanstraat
Closed Mon. Open Tue-Sun 11am-5pm
Admission €7.50

Built in the early 1920s, this social housing apartment complex is at once a prime example of the Amsterdam School of architecture, and a museum dedicated to it. Designed by Michel de Klerk in a brick expressionist style—and vaguely resembling the outlines of ship—the building reflects the architectural style used throughout many of Amsterdam's outer boroughs. It houses 102 dwellings, a small meeting hall and a post office, which is now the museum.

Slow Food on a Boat

Pont 13

 Haparandadam 50
+31 20 770 2722
pont13.nl
Bus 22 48 to Oostzaanstraat
Open daily 5pm-1am. Open during the summer only; refer to website for details

If dining *sur l'eau* sounds like a tempting prospect, make it a priority to visit Pont 13, an excellent slow food venue in a converted boat on the banks of the IJ. During the warmer months, Pont 13 whips up a culinary storm chock full of meats roasted on the spit, fresh grilled fish and sustainably sourced vegetables. An absolute delight for the palate, the unique ambience of the restaurant-boat and its modern maritime décor cannot be beat.

Nose-to-Tail Bistro

Fa. Speijkervet

 Admiraal de Ruijterweg 79
+31 20 223 6004
speijkervet.nl
Admiraal de Ruijterweg **12 13 14**, Jan
Evertsenstraat/de With **7**
Closed Mon. Open Tue-Fri 2pm-
midnight; Sat/Sun 11am-midnight

With its nose-to-tail locavore ethos, uncompromising culinary standards and Northern Bistro flair, Fa. Speijkervet has quickly become an Oud-West foodie hotspot. Brothers Matthias and Lennard van der Nagel source organic ingredients locally, spinning them into innovative and traditional Northern European dishes, the likes of stuffed rabbit filled with cabbage, lemon beans and spek, or steak and kidney pie. Fa. Speijkervet operates a continuous kitchen, making flexible dining a reality.

Pizza on the Canal

Bar Spek

 Admiraal de Ruijterweg 1
+31 20 618 8102

barspek.nl

Willem de Zwijgerlaan **12 13 14**

Open daily. Mon-Thu 8am-1am; Fri/
Sat 9am-2am; Sun 9am-1am

Specialising in fresh baked thin crust pizza, Bar Spek's canal-side terrace, cosy industrial-lamped interior and trendy, relaxed crowd are indicative of the Oud West's ascent within the Amsterdam circuit. Far from limiting itself to its eponymous bacon, Spek is also an excellent choice for *ontbeijt* (breakfast), preferably taken on the comfy mint green sofa.

Noord

—Diamond in the Rough

Until the early 2000s, Amsterdam's north was largely off the radar for all but those who lived there—only Shell's stark 1966 Overhoeks Tower seemed to prove to Amsterdammers that there was indeed life on the northern shores of the IJ. Today, the area is brimming with activity, as media companies move into former industrial warehouses and developers jockey for roles in recreating Amsterdam's newest neighbourhood.

For centuries, the North consisted of only a narrow peninsula across the IJ from the city proper. In the late 19th century, more land was reclaimed for mixed-use development, but the area's isolated—and cheap—land proved more attractive to heavy industry and soon developed into an important hub for petrochemicals and shipbuilding. Shipbuilding had disappeared by the 1980s, its grounds taken over first by artists and more recently converted into office space for the creative sector. In the past decade, the focus has shifted to the former Shell research centre not far from Buiksloterweg, the Noord's main ferry link to central Amsterdam, which is being developed into a new waterfront neighbourhood, Overhoeks. The über-contemporary Eye Film Institute (p97) opened in 2012 as one of the area's first new occupants.

In contrast to the modern waterside developments, the Noord also has a number of picturesque corners with an almost unspoilt feel. Explored by foot or bike, these cores of the former villages that were engulfed by the city, such as Nieuwendammerdijk, feel far removed from Amsterdam's busy centre just across the water.

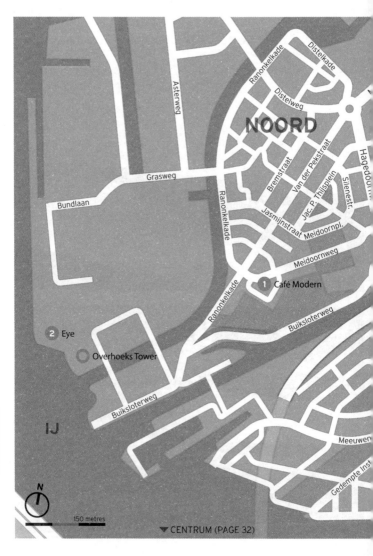

NOORD

IJ

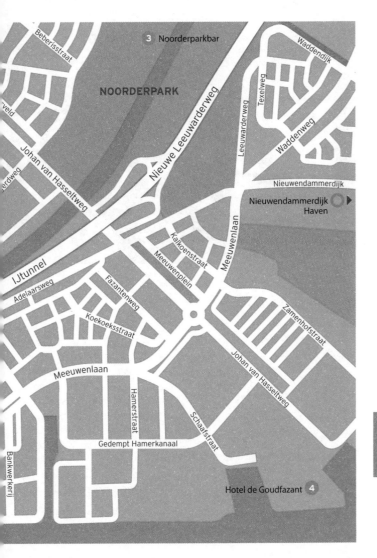

3 Noorderparkbar

Waddendijk

Beberisstraat

NOORDERPARK

Nieuwe Leeuwarderweg

Leeuwarderweg

Texelweg

Waddenweg

veld

Johan van Hasseltweg

erdweg

Nieuwendammerdijk

Nieuwendammerdijk
Haven

IJtunnel

Kalkoenstraat

Meeuwenlaan

Meeuwenplein

Adelaarsweg

Fazantenweg

Koekoeksstraat

Zamenhofstraat

Meeuwenlaan

Johan van Hasseltweg

Hamerstraat

Schaafstraat

Bankwerkerij

Gedempt Hamerkanaal

Hotel de Goudfazant **4**

50s Chic Dining

Café Modern

1 Meidoornweg 2
+31 20 494 0684

modernamsterdam.nl

Ferry to Veer Buiksloterweg from Amsterdam Centraal

Closed Sun. Open Mon-Sat from 7pm. Lunch by Jacques Jour Mon-Sat noon-2pm; Sun 10.30am-4pm

Doubles from €85/night incl. tax

Housed in an old bank building and dressed up in 1950s style, Café Modern offers inspiring gastronomy in the midst of Amsterdam's North. The five-course menu is consistently fresh, creative and excellent, fusing traditional elements of Continental cuisine with exciting new twists. A buzzy, artistic vibe predominates. Take advantage of Café Modern's location within close walking distance of the ferry terminus from Amsterdam Centraal and combine with a film and drinks at the nearby Eye Film Institute (p97).

Best in Film and Architecture

Eye

2 IJpromenade 1
+31 20 589 1400
eyefilm.nl
Ferry to Veer Buiksloterweg from
Amsterdam Centraal
Open daily. Sun-Thu 10am-10pm; Fri/
Sat 10am-11pm
Admission €10

The Eye Film Institute is the first of
Amsterdam's cultural institutions
to have made the move over the
IJ to the city's northern banks.
Vienna's Delugan Meissel Architects
transformed the plot into a
stunning spaceship-like structure,
complete with an excellent
independent cinema, exhaustive
film collection, and jaw dropping
bar and restaurant with cinematic
views of the city centre. With a
vocation to foster a strong film
culture in the Netherlands, the
Eye curates a constant stream of
exhibitions and educational events
exploring the multifaceted nature
of the medium.

Design Driven Coffee

Noorderparkbar

 Floraparkweg
+31 20 737 0457

noorderparkbar.nl

Bus **32 33** to Johan van Hasseltweg
from Amsterdam Centraal
Closed Mon/Tue. Open Wed-Sun
11am-7pm. Open during the summer
only; refer to website for details

Located in the midst of Noord
Amsterdam's largest park,
Noorderparkbar provides a
welcome pit stop for coffee, drinks
and snacks in this otherwise largely
residential part of the city. The café
sprung up as the result of a bottom-
up initiative by two Amsterdam
architecture practices, SLA and
Overtreders W, who designed,
funded and completed the project.
The café's structure and interior—
except for the espresso machine—
are built entirely from recovered
materials.

Glamorous Secluded Dining

Hotel de Goudfazant

4 Aambeeldstraat 10 H
+31 20 636 5170
hoteldegoudfazant.nl
Bus **32 33** to Johan van Hasseltweg
from Amsterdam Centraal
Closed Mon. Open Tue-Sun from
6pm

Set among the ruggedly forlorn shrubbery, warehouses and quays of the northern IJ, de Goudfazant's sumptuous French fusion cuisine, excellent wine list and unparalleled dressed-up-industrial garage setting make this one of the city's most successful dining rooms. The restaurant benefits from its slightly remote location by attracting a clientele willing to make the extra effort for their epicurean supper. Night views of central Amsterdam twinkling away in the distance are hazily stunning.

Essentials

Airport Transfer

Amsterdam's Schiphol Airport (AMS), located 15 km southwest of the city centre, is the main airport of both Amsterdam and the Netherlands. Opened in 1916 as a military airfield it is today the fourth busiest airport in Europe.

The most comfortable way into central Amsterdam is by taxi, of which there are plenty outside Arrivals. A taxi ride to Leidseplein on the edge of the canal belt will take about 25 minutes and cost €40 or more.

Schiphol's main terminal is located directly on top of the mainline rail tracks into Amsterdam; a single ticket to Amsterdam Centraal (€4) can be used on any train into the city. The travel time is 17 mins and trains depart approximately every 10 mins. Trains into Amsterdam run on different tracks, so it's easiest to ask train staff which platform the next train to Amsterdam Centraal will depart from.

Taxis

The city centre's narrow streets, limited by canals, tram tracks and bike lanes, mean that taxis are often not the quickest or easiest way of getting from A to B. Amsterdam's taxis are also among the most expensive in Europe and, despite recent efforts to clean things up, there are still occasionally dodgy practices, such as overcharging.

Taxis are not permitted to stop everywhere for pick-up or drop-off, but most major stations and squares have taxi ranks. Beginning in 2014, taxi ranks are scheduled to be clearly marked by a column topped by a lit "T".

The largest taxi company is Taxicentrale Amsterdam (tcataxi.nl, +31 20 777 7777). A ride from Amsterdam Centraal to the Museumsplein, just south of the canal belt, will take around 15 mins and cost €15, if traffic permits.

Public Transport

Amsterdam's trams are unique in being a major capital city's primary means of transport. Most of the 16 lines, each numbered and coded with a unique square colour code, operate from about 5.30am in the morning to 0.30am at night. Frequencies range from intervals of a few minutes during rush hours, especially when several lines share the same track, to as much as every 10 mins or more in the late evening.

A single disposable ticket valid for one hour on all public transport, including interchanges, costs €2.80. Unlimited travel passes ("OV-chipkaart") for periods ranging from 1 day/24 hrs (€7.50) to 7 days/168 hours (€32) can be purchased at newsstands. See p106 for a tram and metro map.

Amsterdam's less well-known Metro, opened in 1977, primarily connects the outer suburbs with Centraal station in the centre. The ferries from Centraal station to Noord (p92) operate at short intervals and are free of charge.

Tipping

Similar to elsewhere in Europe, tipping is not generally expected but appreciated for good service. A 5-10% tip is common in restaurants, as is rounding up by one or two euros or leaving the change in taxis, cafés and bars. At times, a service charge may already be included in the bill.

Safety

Amsterdam is a wealthy city in a country with a generous welfare state, but it is also a global city with its share of big city crime. On a high level, the pretty, wealthy and dense inner city, including the *De Wallen* red-light district, is safer than the less well-off outskirts, though petty criminals do of course prefer to frequent the same bustling areas enjoyed by tourists.

Index

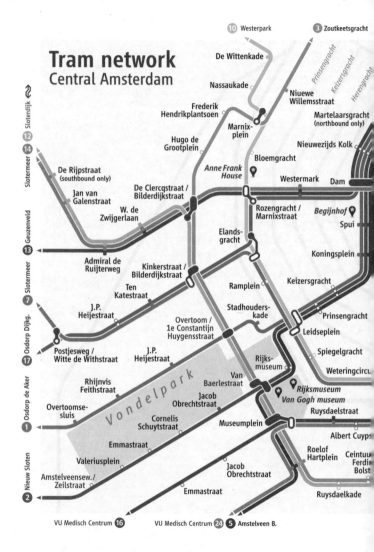

Tram network
Central Amsterdam

Westerpark 10
Zoutkeetsgracht 3
De Wittenkade
Nassaukade
Niuewe Willemsstraat
Frederik Hendrikplantsoen
Marnix-plein
Martelaarsgracht (northbound only)
Hugo de Grootplein
Nieuwezijds Kolk
Bloemgracht
Anne Frank House
Westermark
Dam
De Clercqstraat / Bilderdijkstraat
Rozengracht / Marnixstraat
Begijnhof
Spui
Elands-gracht
Koningsplein
Admiral de Ruijterweg
Kinkerstraat / Bilderdijkstraat
Ramplein
Keizersgracht
Ten Katestraat
Prinsengracht
J.P. Heijestraat
Overtoom / 1e Constantijn Huygensstraat
Stadhouders-kade
Leidseplein
Postjesweg / Witte de Withstraat
J.P. Heijestraat
Rijks-museum
Spiegelgracht
Weteringcircu
Rhijnvis Feithstraat
Van Baerlestraat
Rijksmuseum Van Gogh museum
Overtoomse-sluis
Jacob Obrechtstraat
Ruysdaelstraat
Cornelis Schuytstraat
Museumplein
Albert Cuyps
Emmastraat
Roelof Hartplein
Ceintuu Ferdi Bolst
Valeriusplein
Jacob Obrechtstraat
Amstelveensew. / Zeilstraat
Emmastraat
Ruysdaelkade

Sloterdijk
12
14
Slotermeer
Geuzenveld
13
Slotermeer
7
Osdorp Dijkg.
17
Osdorp de Aker
1
Nieuw Sloten
2

De Rijstraat (southbound only)
Jan van Galenstraat
W. de Zwijgerlaan

VU Medisch Centrum 16
VU Medisch Centrum 24
5 Amstelveen B.

Vondelpark

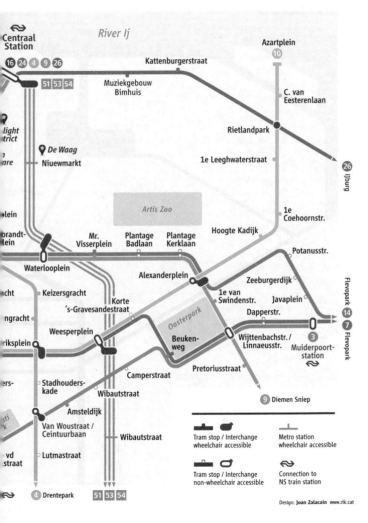

Central Station

River Ij

16 24 4 9 26

51 53 54

Azartplein
10

Kattenburgerstraat

Muziekgebouw
Bimhuis

C. van
Eesterenlaan

light
strict

De Waag
Niuewmarkt

Rietlandpark

1e Leeghwaterstraat

26 IJburg

lein

Artis Zoo

1e
Coehoornstr.

brandt-
lein

Mr.
Visserplein

Plantage
Badlaan

Plantage
Kerklaan

Hoogte Kadijk

Waterlooplein

Potanusstr.

Alexanderplein

cht

Keizersgracht

Korte
's-Gravesandestraat

Zeeburgerdijk

1e van
Swindenstr.

Javaplein

ngracht

Oosterpark

Dapperstr.

14 Flevopark

rikplein

Weesperplein

Beuken-
weg

Wijttenbachstr. /
Linnaeusstr.

3

7 Flevopark

ers-

Stadhouders-
kade

Camperstraat

Pretoriusstraat

Muiderpoort-
station

Wibautstraat

9 Diemen Sniep

Amsteldijk

Van Woustraat /
Ceintuurbaan

Wibautstraat

Tram stop / Interchange
wheelchair accessible

Metro station
wheelchair accessible

vd
straat

Lutmastraat

Tram stop / Interchange
non-wheelchair accessible

Connection to
NS train station

4 Drentepark

51 53 54

Design: **Joan Zalacain** www.zlk.cat

TRAM & METRO MAP   PAGE 107

Credits

Published by Analogue Media, LLC
244 5th Avenue, Suite 2446, New York, NY 10001, United States

Edited by Alana Stone
Layout & Production by Stefan Horn

For more information about the Analogue Guides series, or to find out about availability and purchase information, please visit analogueguides.com

First Edition 2014
ISBN: 978-0-9838585-7-7

Text, book design and layout copyright © 2014 Analogue Media

Every effort has been made to ensure the accuracy of the information in this publication. However, some details are subject to change. The publisher cannot accept responsibility for any loss, injury, inconvenience, or other consequences arising from the use of this book.

Typefaces: Neutraface 2, Myriad Pro and Interstate
Paper: Munken Lynx

Printed in Barcelona by Agpograf, S.A.

Analogue Media would like to thank all contributing venues, designers, manufacturers, agencies and photographers for their kind permission to reproduce their work in this book.

Cover design by Dustin Wallace
Proofread by John Leisure
Tram network Central Amsterdam © Joan Zalacain

All photography credited to the listed venues unless stated otherwise:

<u>Canal Belt</u> (9/17/18) Stefan Horn (21) photo: Huis Marseille, 2013 (22) Peter Cox as photographer and Akinci (23) Mo Schalkx/Property Of... (26/27) Stefan Horn

<u>Centrum & Docklands</u> (31) Stefan Horn (36) 1 star room by Christoph Seyferth - photo: Rob 't Hart (37) Hotel Droog, The one and only bedroom by droog, www.hoteldroog.com (38) Stefan Horn (39) Bart Nieuwenhuijs (40) Stefan Horn (41) Henny Boogert/Athenaeum Boekhandel (42) Stefan Horn (45) Erik van Gurp

<u>Jordaan</u> (47/50/51) Stefan Horn (52) Jasper Faber (53) Stefan Horn (54) Debbie Trouerbach (55) Tim Boelaars (56) Stefan Horn (57) Bob Bronshoff (58) Stefan Horn

<u>De Pijp</u> (61) Stefan Horn (68) Stefan Horn (69) Cathelijne van de Lande (70) Ronald Hoeben (71) Janus van den Eijnden

<u>Oud-Zuid</u> (73) Stefan Horn (76) Gallery of Honour. Photo credit: Iwan Baan. Image Courtesy of Rijksmuseum (77) Stefan Horn

<u>Oud-West</u> (79) Stefan Horn (84) Jelle Rietveld (85) Ewout Huibers x ...,staat creative agency (86) Arjen Veldt (87) fotopuur.nl (88) Roel Vincken - Urban Capture (90) Stefan Horn

<u>Noord</u> (93) Stefan Horn (96) Janus van den Eijnden (98) Shinji Otani

About the Series

—A Modern Take on Simple Elegance

Analogue Guides is a series of curated city guidebooks featuring unique, high quality, low key venues—distilled through the lens of the neighbourhood.

Each neighbourhood is complemented by a concise set of listings, including restaurants, cafés, bars, hotels and serendipitous finds, all illustrated with photographs. The listings are supplemented by custom designed, user-friendly maps to facilitate navigation of the cityscape. Venues featured in the guides score high on a number of factors, including locally sourced food, tasteful design, a sophisticated and relaxed atmosphere and independent ownership.

Analogue Guides are designed to complement the internet during pre-travel preparation and smartphones for on-the-ground research. Premium photography and a select choice of venues provide an ideal starting point for pre-travel inspiration. At your destination, the guides serve as portable manuals with detailed neighbourhood maps and clear directions.

The result: a compact, efficient, effervescent manual celebrating the ingenuity of the contemporary metropolis.